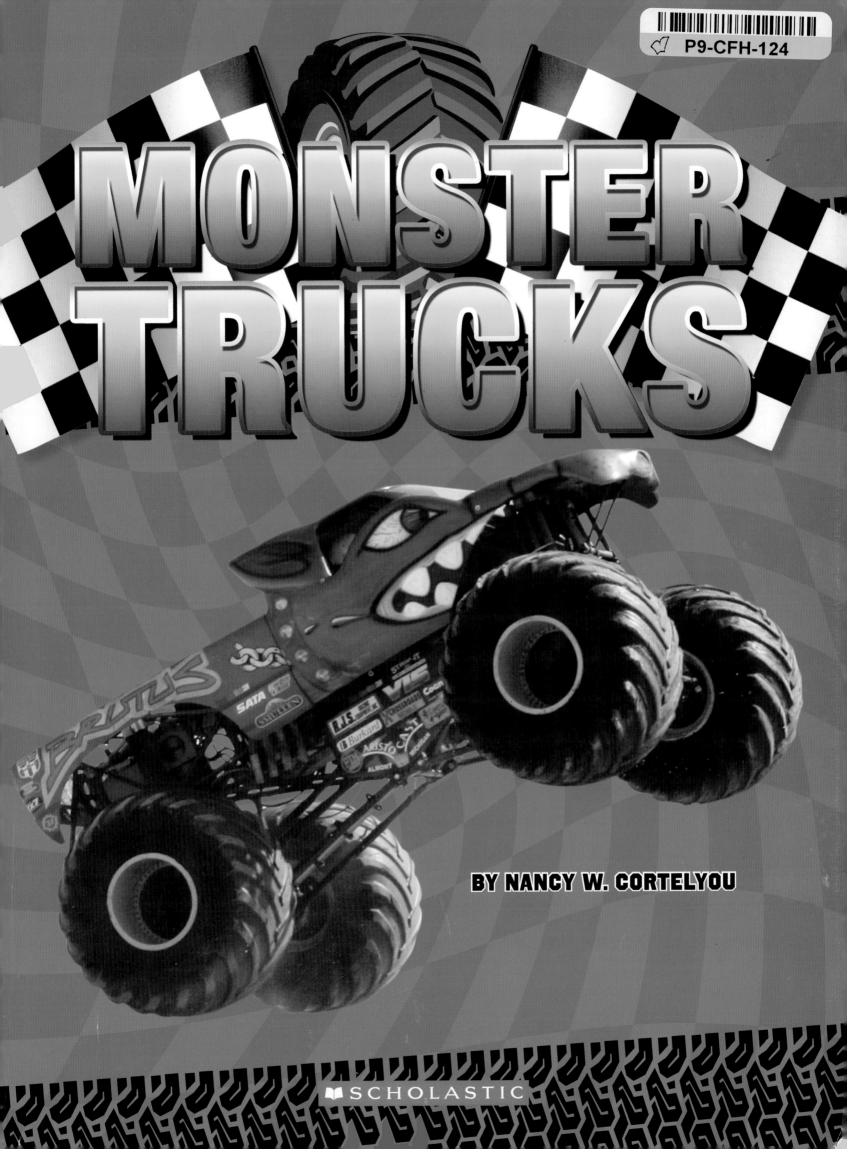

MONSTER TRUCKS

BY NANCY W. CORTELYOU

SCHOLASTIC

an imprint of

SCHOLASTIC

www.scholastic.com

© 2011 becker&mayer! LLC

Published by Tangerine Press, an imprint of Scholastic Inc., 557 Broadway, New York, NY 10012; Scholastic Canada Ltd., Markham, Ontario; Scholastic Australia Pty. Ltd, Gosford NSW; Scholastic New Zealand Ltd., Greenmount, Auckland

Monster Trucks is produced by becker&mayer!, LLC.
11120 NE 33rd Place, Suite 101
Bellevue, WA 98004
www.beckermayer.com

Special thanks to Ross Z. Bonar, TheMonsterBlog.com; Stephanie Cotnoir and the team at avengerracing.com; Jim Allen; Joe Sylvester Motorsports; Don Frankish; Tod and KJ at Uncle Tod Motorsports; Patti Jucha; Ron and Shelley Kujat; Brian Manson; Ranger Joe Cypher; Dan Galvis; Larry Quick; Kaila Savage; Doug and Brenda Noelke; Tracey Gemmel for the photo of Stephanie Cotnoir on page 30; Randy Moore at War Wizard Racing; Jim and Monica Mace; Petri Motorsports; Tod Weston, Greg Winchenbach, and the team at Bottom Feeder Motor Sports; Dan DeChiaro; Paul Shafer and Shafer Motorsports; Steve Sims and the Stone Crusher team; and Perrin Motor Sports.

Written by Nancy W. Cortelyou
Edited by Betsy Henry Pringle
Designed by Rosanna Villarta Brockley
Design assistance by Cortny Helmick
Photo research by Zena Chew and Katie del Rosario
Production management by Jennifer Marx

Photo credits: Front cover: Spike © Stephanie Cotnoir and the team at www.avengerracing.com. Title Page: Brutus © Stephanie Cotnoir. Page 3: Line of trucks © Ross Z. Bonar, TheMonsterBlog.com. Page 4: Bigfoot © Shutterstock. Page 5: Bigfoot © Shutterstock. Page 6: Crushing cars and elephant © Dreamstime. Page 7: Bear Foot © Ross Z. Bonar. Page 8: Airborne Ranger © Ross Z. Bonar. Page 9: Big Pete © Jack Sullivan/Alamy; Team Scream © Stephanie Cotnoir. Page 10: Bad Habit © Joe Sylvester Motorsports. Page 11: American Guardian © Ross Z. Bonar. Page 12-13: All photos © Stephanie Cotnoir. Page 14: Jurassic Attack © Don Frankish, Frankish Enterprises. Page 15: Backdraft © Dreamstime. Page 16-17: Bad Habit © Joe Sylvester Motorsports. Page 18: Pit party (top and bottom) © Ross Z. Bonar; man in sunglasses © Stephanie Cotnoir. Page 19-21: All photos © Stephanie Cotnoir. Page 22: Time Flys © Jim Allen, TheMonsterBlog.com. Page 23: Crushstation © Ross Z. Bonar. Page 24: Heart Breaker © Ross Z. Bonar. Page 25: Big Dawg © Big Dawg and Tail Gator Monster Truck Racing. Page 26: Toxic © Toxic Monster Truck Racing by Petri Motorsports. Page 27: All photos © Ross Z. Bonar. Page 28: Jurassic Attack © Ross Z. Bonar. Page 29: Seat and driver in seat © Stephanie Cotnoir; helmet © iStockphoto. Page 30: All photos © Stephanie Cotnoir. Page 31: Kid KJ's Mini Monster Truck, "Monster Bear," © Uncle Tod Motorsports, www.uncletodmotorsports.com. Page 32: Prowler and Reptoid © Ross Z. Bonar. Page 33: Swamp Thing © Dreamstime. Page 34: All photos © iStockphoto. Page 35: Samson © Dan DeChiaro/flickr. Page 36: Scarlet Bandit © Ross Z. Bonar. Page 37: War Wizard © Ross Z. Bonar. Page 38: Red Dragon © Shutterstock. Page 39: All photos © Ron and Shelley Kujat, Shell-Camino Monster Truck. Page 40-42: All photos © Stephanie Cotnoir. Page 43: Stone Crusher © Ross Z. Bonar. Page 44-45: All photos © Ross Z. Bonar. Page 46: Truck switches © Jim Mace's Hawgwild Monster Truck. Page 47: All photos © Ross Z. Bonar. Page 48: All photos © Stephanie Cotnoir. Ghost Ryder gatefold: all photos © Ross Z. Bonar. Critter Corral gatefold: Crushstation, Pouncer, Predator, and Reptoid photos © Ross Z. Bonar; Spike Unleashed photo © Stephanie Cotnoir. Back cover: Avenger © Stephanie Cotnoir.

Printed, manufactured, and assembled in Shenzhen, China

10 9 8 7 6 5 4 3 2 1
ISBN: 978-0-545-38133-8
10518

SUNDAY! SUNDAY! SUNDAY! BE THERE!!!

Pure excitement! That's what it's like to watch monster trucks in action. These heavies jump, fly, spin, and pogo! And if they don't roll over before they're finished, they give the crowd a high-speed victory donut!

The first monster trucks were just regular trucks. Owners raised them up and tricked them out using tractor or industrial parts. Computers are used to build these racers from scratch. These monsters are lighter, but also stronger and faster. And more able to do all those high-flying jumps!

Think you're a hot shoe ready to mash the throttle in a side-by-side? Better learn some monster truck-racing lingo first.

Air: A truck in flight

Cyclone: A high-speed donut

Donut: When a truck spins in circles in one spot

Hot shoe: Top driver

Mash the throttle: To step down hard on the accelerator

Sick air: A truck in *extreme* flight

Side-by-side: Two trucks racing against each other

Steering wheel holder: An inexperienced driver

T-bone: To crash head-on into the side of an obstacle

Wheelie: Lifting the front end of the truck while driving on two back tires

FAST FACTS

Now you're ready for wheelies and rollovers and trucks flying through the air! Check out the *Fast Facts!* throughout this book for more insider lingo, facts, and figures.

BIGFOOT

First things first! Bigfoot is the first-ever monster truck—built in 1974 by monster truck pioneer Bob Chandler. There are now over a dozen Bigfoot Monster Trucks. All of them have a "first" to their name. One Bigfoot truck can even claim to be the first monster truck movie star.

FAST FACTS

Monster truck racing began in the United States and the sport is still most popular in the home of the brave. However, these mighty trucks are racing their way to Europe, Australia, and Latin America.

FAST FACTS

Officially, a monster truck must weigh at least 9,000 pounds (4 t), including the fuel and the driver. Most trucks weigh between 10,000–12,000 pounds (4.5–5.5 t). That's as heavy as an elephant!

BEAR FOOT

Five years went by before Bigfoot had competition—
Bear Foot! Creator Fred Shafer owned two American
Black Bears, Sugar and Spice, that rode in the back
of his truck. People started calling it the bear truck.
So, Fred named his big love, trucks, after his other
love—animals.

AIRBORNE RANGER

Airborne Ranger is the first hand-controlled monster truck. That means its driver can run the rig without foot pedals. This is handy for driver Ranger Joe, whose legs became paralyzed in a car accident. When doctors told him he would never walk again, Joe said, "No way." His physical challenge gave him the idea to design his special monster truck. Now he can walk with a cane—and drive with his hands.

FAST FACTS

Monster truck tires start life as tractor tires. First, the treads are shaved down to produce better traction and less weight. The cutting is done by hand with a razor and can take as long as 50 hours per tire.

FAST FACTS

The sound of a monster truck engine screams like a race car. Why is it so loud? There are no mufflers on these raceway babes.

AMERICAN GUARDIAN

American Guardian's driver celebrates his wins with a fiery flame shooting out the back of the truck! This onboard flame machine is called an afterburner. It's like the afterburner on a jet engine— but much smaller. The huge American eagle painted across American Guardian's hood flies in the air carrying the American flag. The flying eagle must help the driver fly, too. In just six shows, he won six events.

AVENGER

Chrome? Racing Blue? Toxic Green? The fans of this hot-rod-themed racer are on the edge of their stadium seats each year. They can't wait to see what color Avenger will be. The color may change, but its driver—Jim Koehler—doesn't. Avenger is the only truck that has competed in every World Finals since 1999 with the same driver at the wheel.

FAST FACTS

Not all monster trucks achieve the glory of winning Monster Jam events. Of the 500 monster trucks in the world, only 100 or so are racers. The rest are used for promotions, exhibits, and to give fans a "ride" they'll never forget!

BACKDRAFT

Father-and-son team Andy and Jeremy Slifko maintains and drives the fire truck racer Backdraft. Jeremy became the full-time driver in 2009 and beat his father the first time they raced against each other! Jeremy also took home the Monster Jam Rookie of the Year Award his first season out. But, Jeremy's favorite thing? Getting big air in freestyle.

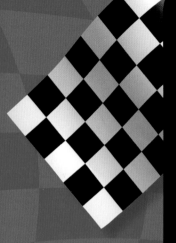

BAD HABIT

The driver: Joe Sylvester III. The truck: Bad Habit. The record: long jump.

When he was five years old, Joe knew he wanted to race monster trucks. At age 26, he's now the youngest independent driver and team owner in the United States. But that's not all. In 2010, he powered Bad Habit to a distance of 208 feet—a new world record!

FAST FACTS

Monster truck drivers like to show off for the crowd, but they take the sport seriously. These professional drivers have lots of experience, and they know how to make racing look easy.

Pit party! Fans are stoked when they attend a preshow pit party that takes place right on the racetrack. This is when they get to meet the drivers, get their autographs, take photos, and eyeball the track.

BOUNTY HUNTER

A bounty hunter is a person who captures a bad guy in exchange for a reward. Bounty Hunter's creator and driver, Jimmy Creten, captures titles in exchange for a life on the monster truck circuit. Jimmy shares the spotlight with his wife, Dawn, who drives Scarlet Bandit. Maybe she's the "outlaw" that Bounty Hunter is chasing!

GHOST RYDER BACKFLIP

Ghost Ryder's driver, Larry Quick, built his monster using a 1968 Mustang Fastback. This speedy duo's claim to fame is the first-ever backflip in front of a live audience. Since this 2009 honor, he backflipped 7 out of 11 tries.

BRUTUS

Brutus started its life as an orange truck with a Greek warrior painted on its hood. For years, fans would tell Chris Bergeron, Brutus's driver, "I have a dog named Brutus." It gave him an idea. In 2004, Brutus entered the ring with a dog's head and pointy ears. The fans went wild! Since then, Brutus has mastered wheelies and is celebrated for its freestyle runs. Good dog!

FAST FACTS

Many monster trucks are covered in large vinyl "stickers" instead of paint. That way, after a crash, the crew can match up the graphics quickly and easily—and get the distinctive truck back out on the raceway.

FAST FACTS

Most monster trucks have two extra-long, nitrogen-filled shock absorbers per tire. Without them, neither the trucks nor the drivers could recover from the jolts delivered by this high-impact sport.

CRUSHSTATION—THE MONSTAH LOBSTAH

Catch this! What do most people think about when they think about Maine? Lobster! That was the inspiration for Greg Winchenbach, the owner and driver of Crushstation. After all, a lobster is a *crustacean (krus-TAY-shun)*. And, like most crustaceans, lobsters have an exoskeleton—a hard body shell that protects its insides, just like a monster truck!

HEART BREAKER

Creating Heart Breaker was a labor of love for female driver Kaila Savage. She started out by helping her fiancé achieve *his* dream of driving. Then, one day, Kaila hopped into the cab and raced—and won! As her pretty pink truck says, she's been "Breaking Hearts at the Finish Line" ever since! One thing Kaila hasn't done—compete against another female driver.

FAST FACTS

In the early days of monster truck racing, drivers had to hoist themselves up onto the front tire. Then, they would climb up into the driver's seat. Nowadays, there's a hatch in the floor of the cab for the driver to climb through. The driver's seat is located in the middle of a monster truck cab! It's easier for the driver to see what he or she is doing from that perch. This design is better for weight balance.

FAST FACTS

Early monster trucks used military axles or school bus axles to support the tires. This construction made the trucks so heavy they could only crawl over the crush cars. Modern monsters use lighter-weight axles that can flex with the truck.

HIGH MAINTENANCE

Wheelie queen, Lil' Miss Dangerous drives High Maintenance. Together, they've been Monster Nationals Freestyle Champions three times. Lil' Miss Dangerous is famous for her cyclones and reverse wheelies—and for the chocolate chip cookies she bakes for her fellow drivers before every show. Then, she wows the crowd with High Maintenance's sweet-scented fuel and pink-and-silver confetti that shoots out the back of the truck!

JURASSIC ATTACK

T. rex or triceratops? Don Frankish, Jurassic Attack's owner, couldn't decide. The result? A blue-textured paint job with three horns, eyes as the side windows, and a spine around its "neck." Former Jurassic Attack driver Kristy Edge made her mark on the monster truck sport as the only female Canadian driver.

Each monster truck driver sits in a custom-molded driver's seat with head and neck restraints. He or she is required to wear a five-point safety harness and racing helmet, as well as a fireproof suit, shoes, and gloves.

FAST FACTS

Want to be a monster truck driver? First, you'll need to learn how to drive! Other requirements: good health and knowledge of the inner and outer workings of a truck. And that's just to make the crew. It'll take you two years to learn how to drive for the team.

MONSTER BEAR

Born in 2003, Kid KJ is the youngest monster truck driver on the raceway. He does it in a half-size monster truck called Monster Bear. Monster Bear has all the same features of a full-size truck, but it's kid-sized. Height: 7 feet (2 m), instead of 11 feet (3.4 m). Weight: 2,500 pounds (1,134 kg), instead of 9,000 pounds (4,082 kg).

PROWLER

Prowler is part of the feline-themed Predator racing team. The owner of this monster mouser runs two other sister trucks named Pouncer and Predator. Predator is thought to be the first custom concept monster truck. That means the body of the truck doesn't just have a fancy paint job. Instead, the body is molded into a shape, like that of an animal. Prowler is just one of three kitties in the house!

FAST FACTS

Dirt dump! It takes a crew three to five days to get a monster truck course ready for racing. Event companies own dirt in every major city. Dump trucks make hundreds of trips to deliver the dirt before each show can begin.

WELCOME TO THE MONST TRUCK CRITTER CORRAL

Get along little doggies, and kitties, and alligators, and . . . !

CRUSHSTATION

TER

PREDATOR

POUNCER

FAST FACTS

The crush cars—vans, buses, ambulances, motor homes, and airplanes—that monster trucks flatten into pancakes are purchased from local junkyards. All are returned after each event.

SCARLET BANDIT

Dawn Creten, the driver of this red-hot number, is one of the few females in the sport. And she is not the only driver in the family—her husband, Jimmy Creten, drives Bounty Hunter. In 2003, Scarlet Bandit beat out fan favorite Maximum Destruction in a *photo finish*. A photo finish is when a race is really close and the naked eye can't tell who won. The judges use a photograph to see who came in first.

PREDATOR

SPIKE

TOID

REPTOID

SAMSON

The gigantic arms of Samson have powerful biceps that break through 3-D chains. The muscles—and the brains—behind the Samson monster truck is Dan Patrick. He owns the truck and a shop that builds monster truck chassis. A "Patrick Chassis" is the frame in many of the monster trucks Samson competes against.

FAST FACTS

Monster trucks can reach speeds of up to 70 mph (112.6 km/h) at a stretch, but they are really built for short bursts of speed. Their engines average about 1,500 horsepower (1,100 kW) to move those tires! A regular car needs about 200 horsepower (147 kW).

FAST FACTS

Monster truck tires must be 66 inches high (168 cm). That's as tall as a refrigerator! A monster truck team goes through about eight tires a year—two full sets for just one truck.

SHELL-CAMINO

"Girls rock!" says Shell-Camino driver Shelley Kujat. She started driving a monster truck to show girls they can do anything they want. Shelley considered racing cars, but didn't like the idea of being so close to the ground. When she's not working the raceway in Shell-Camino, Shelley's driving a FedEx delivery truck.

SPIKE UNLEASHED

Siberian Husky dogs have two favorite pastimes—digging and howling. With blue eyes and pointy ears, Spike Unleashed looks like a Husky. He acts like one, too! He digs holes in the dirt when he gets those monster trucks spinning. And boy, does his engine howl! Spike isn't the only dog in the house. He shares the spotlight with his Team Scream brother Brutus. Check out Brutus on page 20.

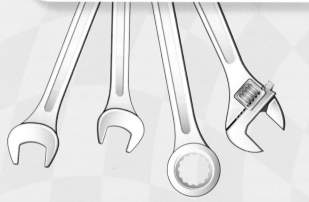

FAST FACTS

Monster trucks are fueled by methanol—a corn-based racing alcohol that works better with the high horsepower of these mega-vehicles. Methanol still gets burned up quickly. Most monster trucks can travel only 100 feet per gallon.

STONE CRUSHER

The stone-crushing world of Steve Sims changed forever when monster driver Dennis Anderson entered his stone shop. Dennis wanted new countertops. Steve told the owner of the world's most recognizable monster truck that he'd barter for services: He'd deliver the countertops if Anderson would bring Grave Digger to his son's birthday party. Deal! Steve soon became a fierce competitor with his own truck, Stone Crusher. His crew won the Team of the Year award in both 2008 and 2009.

TAILGATOR

Tailgator's creator, Doug Noelke, grew up in St. Louis, home of Bigfoot. He often rode past Bigfoot's shop and dreamed about owning a monster truck of his own. His dream came true, twice! First, he remodeled an old Ford Bronco he found in the woods. Then, came Tailgator. Along the way, Doug has been Rookie, Driver, and Sportsman of the Year running his monster alligator.

FAST FACTS

Freestyle is the part of a monster truck show when the trucks do stunts and tricks, instead of race. Stunts include high jumps, wheelies, and donuts.

FAST FACTS

Every monster truck has three safety shutoffs, called kill switches. These are used to shut down the engine when there is a safety concern. One kill switch is in the cab, and one is on the outside of the truck. There is also a RII (remote ignition interrupter) controlled by a rally official.

WAR WIZARD

"Set your goals, work hard, and never let anyone tell you that you cannot do it!" War Wizard racer Randy Moore's beliefs earned him a spot in the *Guinness Book of World Records*. In 2005, he set out to beat the monster truck speed record. He did it with a speed of 84.382 mph (135.8 km/h). Step aside, Bigfoot #14. Your 1999 record is broken by 15 mph (24.1 km/h). That's fast!

WRECKING CREW

Caution everybody! Wrecking Crew is on the racetrack. This machine of destruction started life in Detroit, the Motor City. Originally, it just filled in for its Team Scream brothers (Avenger, Brutus, and Spike Unleashed) when they couldn't make a show. Now, Wrecking Crew is a full-time monster truck. What gets its driver pumped? The sound of the fans and the roar of the engine!